THE MEXICAN
DRUG WAR

Essential Issues

The Mexican

Drug War

by Courtney Farrell

Content Consultant
Sanho Tree, Fellow
Institute for Policy Studies

ABDO
Publishing Company

CREDITS

Published by ABDO Publishing Company, 8000 West 78th Street, Edina, Minnesota 55439. Copyright © 2012 by Abdo Consulting Group, Inc. International copyrights reserved in all countries. No part of this book may be reproduced in any form without written permission from the publisher. The Essential Library™ is a trademark and logo of ABDO Publishing Company.

Printed in the United States of America,
North Mankato, Minnesota
062011
092011

Editor: Amy Van Zee
Copy Editor: Jennifer Joline Anderson
Cover Design: Marie Tupy
Interior Design and Production: Kazuko Collins

Library of Congress Cataloging-in-Publication Data
Farrell, Courtney.
  The Mexican drug war / by Courtney Farrell.
    p. cm. -- (Essential issues)
  Includes bibliographical references and index.
  ISBN 978-1-61783-136-2
  1. Drug traffic--Mexico--Juvenile literature. 2. Drug traffic--Mexican-American Border Region--History--Juvenile literature. 3. Drug traffic--Social aspects--Mexico--Juvenile literature. I. Title.
  HV5840.M4F37 2011
  363.450972--dc22

                    2011016136

TABLE OF CONTENTS

Chapter 1	Drugs, Guns, and Money	6
Chapter 2	The History of the Cartels	16
Chapter 3	The Crackdown	26
Chapter 4	Kidnappings	36
Chapter 5	Corruption	46
Chapter 6	How the Drug War Affects Youth	54
Chapter 7	The Mexican Drug War and the United States	64
Chapter 8	The Mexican Drug War on US Soil	74
Chapter 9	No Easy Solutions	82
Timeline		96
Essential Facts		100
Glossary		102
Additional Resources		104
Source Notes		106
Index		109
About the Author		112

A police officer stands near the entrance to a drug smuggling tunnel that begins in Mexico and travels approximately 1,000 feet (305 m) into Southern California.

DRUGS, GUNS, AND MONEY

uan José Soriano was deputy commander of the police in Tecate, Mexico, a scenic desert town on the US–Mexico border. The town's location made it a favorite route for traffickers smuggling drugs into California, and Soriano made it his job to stop them. His relentless pursuit of the *narcos,* or drug dealers, meant he had powerful enemies. Both the wealthy drug lords and the corrupt officials on their payrolls wanted him out of the way. In 2005, Soriano was relegated to a desk job amidst rumors that some shadowy underworld figure had pulled strings to put him there. "They took away his wings. They weren't ready for where he was going," said an unidentified US law enforcement officer.[1]

In 2007, Tecate's new mayor, Donaldo Peñalosa, brought Soriano back in an attempt to rein in the traffickers, who were organized into violent gangs. These drug-trafficking organizations (DTOs) are commonly called drug cartels. Two days after Soriano's promotion, a drug-sniffing dog led a US Border Patrol agent to a cargo container not far north of the Mexican border. Inside the cargo container, the officer encountered an armed man stacking bundles of marijuana. The gunman quickly darted into a hole in the ground—a tunnel to the Mexican side of the border. The Border Patrol officer telephoned Soriano. They needed to know where the other opening of the tunnel was, and the operation had to happen quickly—before the gangsters had time to take their drugs and disappear.

Marijuana

Marijuana comes from a plant called canna-bis, which contains the psychoactive chemical tetrahydrocannabinol (THC). Users commonly smoke marijuana, but cannabis extracts can also be added to foods. When THC enters the body, it binds to sites in the brain called cannabinoid receptors. These receptors control brain functions including pleasure, learn-ing, and perception of the passage of time. Chronic users can be at risk for short-term memory loss, lung cancer, and emphysema.

In some states, mari-juana is legal for medical use by patients who suf-fer from chronic pain or nausea. For those expe-riencing weight loss as a result of chemotherapy or an illness, marijuana might be prescribed because it stimulates appetite. However, the medical benefits of mari-juana are often questioned or weighed against the potential problems associ-ated with marijuana use.

Soriano knew this was a dangerous situation. The tunnel was worth millions of dollars to drug traffickers, and they would kill to defend it. Another complication was the presence of corrupt officers on the Tecate police force. Cartels typically use threats and bribes to gain the cooperation of police, so Soriano did not have many officers he could trust. He mustered his men and confiscated their cell phones, hoping to prevent a traitor from warning the cartel. After handpicking a few trusted officers, Soriano invented a story about a car chase and sent the rest off on the false alarm.

The officers crossed into the United States and entered the tunnel, alert for a possible ambush. They followed the tunnel back across the border to Mexico. It led to an 80-foot-(24-m-) deep shaft that rose into an abandoned building. The traffickers had fled, but computers and documents they left behind revealed an operation worth tens of millions of dollars.

That night, as deputy commander Soriano slept beside his wife and near his infant daughter, gunmen armed with AK-47 assault rifles burst into his home. Soriano apparently knew the men and begged them not to shoot. They killed him with a barrage of gunfire that barely missed his baby daughter in the crib behind him.

Afterward, residents of Tecate whispered that it was the police who murdered him, although there was no evidence to prove it. Police officers who attended Soriano's funeral talked and laughed disrespectfully during the ceremony, and the deputy commander's photo was never placed on the department's shrine to fallen officers. Back at the tunnel, the incriminating computers and documents mysteriously disappeared, and no suspects were ever arrested.

"It's a shame," said Donald McDermott, a former Border Patrol officer who worked with Soriano. "He was one of the good guys. . . . His untimely demise was a blow to border enforcement on both sides of the border."[2]

THE ILLEGAL DRUG TRADE

Drug trafficking in Mexico and other parts of Latin America has become a dangerous, growing threat. Drug traffickers risk prison and violent death, but the business is a lucrative one. Approximately 70 percent of the illegal drugs that enter the United States come through Mexico, making the drug trade one of that nation's biggest industries.

Cocaine from Mexico

Statistics vary, but experts estimate that approximately 90 percent of the cocaine sold in the United States enters through Mexico.

Exact numbers are not known because of the secretive nature of criminal enterprises, but Mexican narcotics profits range between $3.2 and $9.91 billion per year. Cocaine, marijuana, heroin, and methamphetamine are among the drugs that are smuggled to US users, who spend an estimated $6.6 billion a year on drugs. In return, guns and illegal military-grade weapons are moved south, destined for the private armies of the cartels. Violence in relation to this growing, illegal drug trade has made news headlines as drug cartels battle each other with deadly outcomes.

With such a high potential for profit, trade routes are essential to the success of these groups. The illegal drug trade relies on access to transportation avenues such as highways, ports, and tunnels, as well as the allegiance of officials who are "bought" through bribes to favor one cartel over another. The economic motivations for turf wars are high, and the stakes are raised as rival gangs are willing to do anything to keep their strongholds on certain regions or key law enforcement officials.

LOCAL ECONOMIES

In poverty-stricken areas of Mexico, drug lords are often admired for their

---

Drugs Are a Global Problem

The drug trade is by no means limited to Mexico. Poor and war-torn areas often develop drug-trafficking industries, and Afghanistan is a prime example. Opium is an addictive drug made from the opium poppy, which grows throughout Afghanistan. Opium can be found in morphine, codeine, and other medicines, but heroin is also made from opium. Estimates show that close to 90 percent of the world's heroin is produced in Afghanistan. The money made from the drug trade helps finance the powerful Islamic militia group known as the Taliban and the terrorist group al-Qaeda. And corrupt government officials have a personal interest in making sure the drug trade in that nation stays robust. Additionally, poor citizens turn to growing opium as a means to support their families.

Heroin is expensive globally but cheap on the streets of Afghanistan. Afghan citizens, stressed by war, are turning to drugs for solace. Drugs were traditionally a male indulgence there, but now women are becoming addicted as well. Many are ignorant of the dangers. Opium is often the only "medicine" available to rural families, and some mothers accidentally addict infants by using opium to soothe them. About 3 percent of Afghan adults are now addicted to opium and heroin.

lavish lifestyles and the community services they provide. "They are very generous with the societies of their towns," said Bishop Carlos Aguiar Retes, president of the Mexican Bishops' Conference. He said in some remote towns, drug traffickers, or narcotraffickers, "put up lights, communications, roads, at their own expense. . . . Often they also build a church or a chapel."[3] Such acts of charity win *narcos* the support of locals, who help them evade capture.

Traffickers stimulate local economies through their purchases of mansions, automobiles, and luxury goods, making politicians reluctant to eradicate the trade entirely. However, the wealth associated with the drug trade comes with a human toll. Addiction, loss of productivity, child neglect, violence, and crime are problems among drug users. In Mexico, these problems worsened after the United States increased border security in response to the terrorist attacks of September 11, 2001. With cross-border smuggling routes restricted, traffickers lowered prices and sold their drugs locally. However, the smuggling business is an arms race, and advantages on one side are soon overcome by innovations on the other. Despite the best efforts of

Mexican federal police officers stand near a crime scene in Tijuana in 2009. Tijuana is a center of cartel activity.

the US Border Patrol, drugs and people continue to cross illegally into the United States.

Although individual traffickers reap huge profits, economic analysis reveals that the drug trade costs Mexican society about $4.3 billion per year. This is because investors are wary of starting businesses in corrupt regions, and taxpayers must pay for drug-related expenses such as law enforcement and incarceration.

Drug-Related Crime

Cartels do business in a world where violence, theft, or broken contracts cannot be reported to the police. This is why virtually every cartel has its own security force made up of young men and tough street kids. In recent years, authorities have been dismayed to discover that the cartels are doing business with underworld arms dealers.

Narcos who once carried handguns and hunting rifles now wear bulletproof vests and wield military-grade weapons such as AK-47s, bazookas, and grenades. The police are out-manned, out-gunned, and out-financed. Cartels battle each other, the police, and the Mexican armed forces—and innocent people are caught in the crossfire. Numbers continue to rise, but since 2006, more than 37,000 people have been killed in violence so widespread that it has become known as the Mexican drug war.

Inside a Drug Cartel

Some cartels set rules for members. The notorious la Familia cartel sells drugs, but it forbids its own members to use them. It seems the cartel knows the dangers of drug use. The group also claims religious motivation and uses money to benefit the poor through building schools and public improvements. La Familia's former leader Nazario Moreno González, known as *el Más Loco* (the Craziest), wrote his own bible of sayings and distributed it to his followers. *El Más Loco* was killed in a gun battle with Mexican federal police in December 2010.

*The aftermath of a shootout between cartel members
and the Mexican Navy Special Forces in 2009*

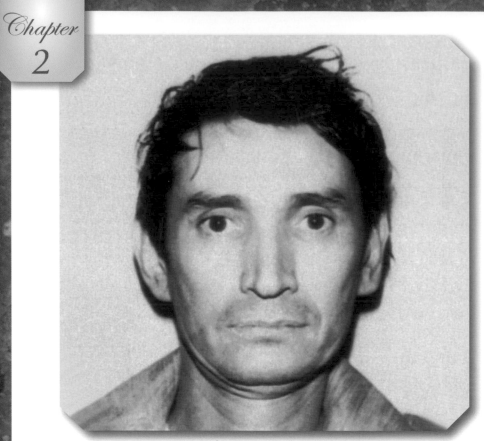

Miguel Ángel Félix Gallardo in 1989

THE HISTORY OF
THE CARTELS

Organized crime along the US–Mexico border began in the 1800s, when gangs of horseback-riding bandits robbed travelers and traded in contraband guns and alcohol. By the 1920s, during America's roaring Jazz Age, US partiers were developing a taste for the opium and marijuana smuggled over the Mexican border. The smugglers' haven was the city of Culiacán, located north of Mazatlán in the Mexican state of Sinaloa. Today, Sinaloa is still "the cradle of the biggest traffickers Mexico has ever known," says former Mexican Federal Police Commander Guillermo González Calderoni.[1] Culiacán's hills are dotted with mansions, and their owners make regular offerings at the shrine of Jesús Malverde, a legendary bandit who has become the idol and patron saint of narcotraffickers.

THE GODFATHER

One of the first modern cartel leaders was Miguel Ángel Félix Gallardo, a Mexican judicial federal police agent born in 1946. Félix Gallardo, dubbed *el Padrino* (the Godfather) was a bodyguard for the governor of Sinaloa. Félix Gallardo

Jesús Malverde

According to legend, Jesús Malverde was a bandit who roamed the state of Sinaloa in the early twentieth century, stealing from the rich and giving to the poor until the police finally killed him in 1909. This Robin Hood–style bandit may never have existed at all, but his worshippers revere him as a saint. They believe that he protects drug traffickers from police, but the opposite may be true. "We send squads out to local hotel and motel parking lots looking for cars with Malverde symbols on the windshield or hanging from the rearview mirror," said Sergeant Rico García of the Houston Police Department's narcotics division. "It gives us a clue that something is probably going on."[2]

met and learned from the powerful drug lord Pedro Áviles. In the 1960s, with support from Áviles, Félix Gallardo and his associates smuggled drugs into the

United States from Sinaloa. In the 1970s, their efforts were hindered by a joint US–Mexico drug control program that used American-supplied planes to spray the toxic herbicide paraquat on marijuana fields in the Mexican states of Sinaloa, Durango, and Chihuahua.

The Paraquat Debate

In the 1970s and 1980s, the herbicide paraquat was used to destroy marijuana and opium poppy fields in Mexico. American-supplied helicopters sprayed the fields while gunmen shot down any farmers who took up arms to protect their crops. Paraquat is highly toxic. A very small amount can kill a person, and inhalation causes bleeding throats and permanent scarring of the lungs. Thousands of Mexican civilians were exposed.

Farmers soon learned that paraquat is color-less and odorless after application, and that exposure to sunlight kills treated plants. After the helicopters departed, farmers quickly har-vested their toxic crop, putting foliage in bags to protect it from the sun. Treated and untreated plants were mixed together and sold.

As a result of the paraquat contamination, US marijuana users reported bad reactions such as vomiting and passing out, and labo-ratories were overwhelmed by requests to test marijuana samples. In 1978, 28 percent of California samples tested positive, while nearly 100 percent of all samples tested by an Illinois lab had traces of the poison. Debate raged over the ethics of spraying the illegal crop. "The U.S. Government has not fulfilled its responsibility to stop poisoning our own citizens," said Sena-tor Charles Percy, a Republican from Illinois.[3]

THE MEXICAN CARTELS ARE BORN

In 1987, Félix Gallardo moved

his cartel to Guadalajara. Through a Honduran cocaine dealer, Gallardo established connections to the Medellín cartel of Colombia and its notorious leader, Pablo Escobar. Crackdowns were making it almost impossible for Colombian cartels to get cocaine-laden boats across the Caribbean Sea to dealers in Florida, so they joined with the Mexican cartels. It was estimated that the Guadalajara cartel was moving two short tons (1.81 metric tons) of cocaine a month into the United States. *El Padrino's* income was estimated at $30 million a month.

At this point, Félix Gallardo headed the only major cartel in Mexico. He feared that one bust could take down his entire organization. So, he divided up the operation, naming a leader for each, but placing himself as their king. It must have seemed like a good idea at the time, but the results were

The Billionaire Drug Lord Pablo Escobar

"Plata o plomo," Pablo Escobar used to say.[4] Silver or lead, money or bullets—that was the choice he gave anyone who got in the way of his multibillion-dollar cocaine business. Escobar's Medellín cartel offered police and politicians bribes, or "silver," to gain their cooperation. Those who refused got a lead bullet instead. Escobar ordered the assassinations of hundreds of people, but many Medellín citizens still loved him. He built schools, parks, churches, sports stadiums, and housing for the poor in his hometown of Medellín. Escobar was shot dead by Colombian security forces in December 1993.

Pablo Escobar was born in 1949. He became involved in the cocaine business in the 1970s.

disastrous. The cartels soon fell into a cutthroat competition for territory, and decades later, the war still shows no sign of ending. Currently, there are approximately eight cartels, but the players change as new groups appear or old ones die off or are absorbed into stronger organizations. "Old cartels don't seem to go away; they just seem to morph into new variants over time," said David Shirk, director of the Trans-Border Institute at the University of San Diego. "There's strong continuity for these organizations, dating back multiple generations of smugglers."[5]

Félix Gallardo's reign came to an end with his 1989 arrest for the torture and killing of US Federal Agent Enrique Camarena Salazar, who had infiltrated the Guadalajara cartel. Police sources report that Félix Gallardo ran his cartel from behind bars until the early 1990s, when he was transferred to a Mexican maximum-security prison.

ONE CARTEL'S DEMISE

Félix Gallardo had seven nephews, the Arellano Félix brothers, and most of them went into the family drug business. The Arellano Félix cartel operated along the border in Tijuana, but in 2008, corpses of members began appearing on the streets. Some had their tongues cut out and others were burned or decapitated.

In August 2008, four headless bodies were found bearing a message: "We are people of the weakened Engineer."[6] Most drug lords have nicknames, and *el Ingeniero* (the Engineer) is Fernando Sánchez

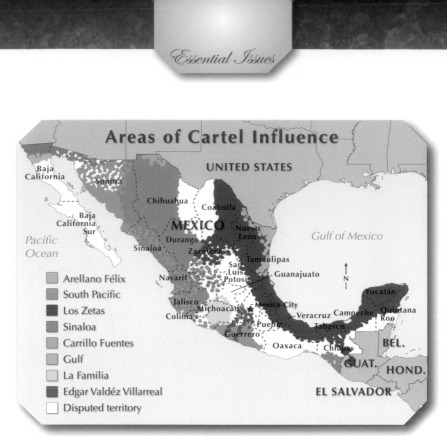

The Mexican cartels are often growing and changing. In early 2011, the Economist *listed the eight major Mexican cartels.*

Arellano, the head of the Arellano Félix cartel. At least 57 more of his people were murdered at the end of September and the beginning of October. Many of the bodies were found with the taunting handwritten notes that are so common in the drug war that they have a name: narco messages.

Authorities interpreted the carnage as a sign that the Arellano Félix cartel was being replaced by a challenger determined to take over its smuggling route across the border into California. About the

Arellano Félix cartel, John Kirby, a former federal prosecutor from San Diego, said, "We are now seeing the tail end. They're losing what was left of their grip on Baja California."[7]

Earlier in 2008, the Arellano Félix cartel had faced civil war when one of its more violent lieutenants, Teodoro García Simental, or *el Teo*, went on a spree of kidnappings. For cartels, kidnappings for ransom are a standard method of fund-raising, but *el Teo* was going too far and bringing pressure upon the group. He refused *el Ingeniero*'s orders to stop. In April 2008, *el Teo* and his minions engaged their former cartel coworkers in a bloody gun battle that left 15 dead. *El Teo* reportedly left the city afterward, but some speculate that the violent murders in fall 2008 are a sign that he is back in Tijuana.

Other signs point to the Sinaloa cartel, which could possibly be working with *el Teo* to move in on the Arellano Félix cartel's Tijuana territory. For example, a banner appeared over a street announcing that "El Mayo and El Chapo are the ones trying to enter Tijuana."[8] *El Mayo* is Ismael Zambada García, and *el Chapo* is his boss, Joaquín Guzmán Loera, the chief of the Sinaloa cartel and

El Chapo

Joaquin Guzmán Loera, also known as *el Chapo*, must have friends in high places. *El Chapo* runs the powerful Sinaloa cartel, which is warring with other cartels over the smuggling route from Ciudad Juárez to El Paso, Texas. In 2010, more than 3,100 people were murdered in Ciudad Juárez. Despite the body count, few Sinaloa members are ever arrested. "It would seem there are a lot of people on the take [taking bribes], including police and military on the local and federal levels," said Howard Campbell, an anthropology professor and cartel expert from the University of Texas–El Paso.[10]

the most-wanted man in Mexico. In early October 2008, Tijuana authorities found eight more decapitated bodies with a note reading, "Here you go, Engineer."[9] The violence has only escalated since then as rival cartels battle for territory and the money and power that go with it.

El Chapo *broke out of a Mexican prison in 2001.*
He is one of the most-wanted criminals in Mexico.

*Felipe Calderón was sworn in as Mexico's president
on December 1, 2006.*

THE CRACKDOWN

*I*n recent decades, Mexican politics and
economics have undergone significant
changes that have fueled the fire of the Mexican
drug war. In 1994, Mexico entered into the North
American Free Trade Agreement (NAFTA) with

the United States and Canada. NAFTA eliminated trade barriers and taxes between the countries so that goods could be more easily traded. In doing so, the trade in illegal substances also became easier. National Public Radio correspondent John Burnett wrote, "With a billion dollars worth of cargo crossing the U.S.-Mexico border every day, free trade is one of the greatest gifts for drug traffickers."[1] Additionally, NAFTA flooded Mexico with cheap commodities from the United States. Peasant farmers in Mexico who were unable to compete were driven off their lands and into cities. To earn a living, some turned to growing or trafficking drugs.

Political changes also contributed to the shifting Mexican society. The Partido Revolucionario Institucional (PRI) held a stronghold on the Mexican government from the time after World War I until 2000. In July of that year, Vicente Fox was elected president of the nation. He was the first non-PRI president in more than 70 years. He intended to eliminate corruption and restore democracy, but his road was challenging. The political changes in some ways weakened the central government, which opened up lower levels of government to corruption.

CALDERÓN'S PLAN

In December 2006, Mexican President Felipe Calderón announced a government crackdown on drug traffickers. The operation was more of a war than a police action, with 45,000 soldiers and 5,000 federal police deployed the first year. The body count has been that of a war too, with at least 37,000 killed between 2006 and 2010. In 2008, Mexico's National Defense Department released a strategy report in which it outlined its four "aspects of combat" against the cartels, which were to "cause the greater number of deaths; create divisionism in their structures; provoke internal confrontations and induce their self-destruction."[2]

Clearly the Mexican government was aware the plan would cause bloodshed, but military involvement seemed to be the lesser of two evils. "What are the alternatives?" asked President Calderón. "Is the alternative to allow organized crime to take over the country?"[3]

Not everyone agrees that the crackdown was the best strategy. "When you have this kind of turf battle going on between rival cartels, the worst thing the state can do is get in the middle of that," said Sanho Tree, director of the Institute for Policy Studies

(IPS), an organization that works for peace, justice, and a healthy environment.[4] Tree believes that eliminating individual drug traffickers does not solve the problem; it creates more violence as survivors compete over vacated territory.

Los Zetas

Sometimes attempts to solve a problem backfire, making the problem worse. This happened in the 1990s, when Mexican soldiers from the Airmobile Special Forces Group (GAFE in its Spanish initials) were trained by US Special Forces personnel at Fort Bragg, North Carolina. "They were given map reading courses, communications, standard Special Forces training, light to heavy weapons, machine guns and automatic weapons," said former Special Forces commander Craig Deare.[5]

The training was intended to prepare elite Mexican soldiers to take on the cartels, but there was a flaw in

Migrants Killed by Drug Gang

On August 24, 2010, 18-year-old Ecuadorian Luis Freddy Lala Pomavilla arrived at a highway checkpoint, bleeding from gunshot wounds to the face and neck. He was the only survivor of a group of 73 migrants from Central and South America who were kidnapped by los Zetas in San Fernando, Mexico. The gang members robbed the migrants and then attempted to recruit them, offering them money to become assassins. When the migrants refused, they were put up against the wall and shot. After the shooting, Lala Pomavilla survived by pretending to be dead.

the system. Mexican soldiers receive very low wages, and consequently, their desertion rate is quite high. Modern cartels offer bribes and make threats, and 25 percent of GAFE soldiers leave their posts before their tours of duty are finished. Many of them end up working for the cartels.

For example, in the mid-1990s, a small group of GAFE soldiers deserted to become los Zetas, the private security force of the Gulf cartel. The group recruited by offering soldiers more money than they could make legally. With their formal training, los Zetas became a formidable force. They worked primarily as hit men for the Gulf cartel until 2010, when they broke off and started their own organization. This ignited a turf war across the states of Tamaulipas and Nuevo Leon. "The Zetas have obviously assumed the role of being the No. 1 organization responsible for the majority of the homicides, the narcotic-related homicides, the beheadings, the kidnappings, the extortions that take place in Mexico," said Ralph Reyes, the US Drug Enforcement Administration's chief for Mexico and Central America.[6]

Mexican cartel leaders once followed a code of conduct reminiscent of the 1950s Italian-American

Mafia. Battles were between men, and women and children were never intentionally harmed. This all changed when los Zetas arrived. Opponents' families, and even random citizens, are killed whenever los Zetas want to make a point. Rival cartels quickly began to copy their merciless style. "At one time, it was considered bad form to kill pregnant women, but not any more," said Mexico-based journalist Kristen Bricker.[7] In January 2011, one of the founders of los Zetas, Flavio Méndez Santiago, or *el Amarillo* (the Yellow One) was arrested on human trafficking charges.

A Record Bust

In 2007, a police raid on a Mexico City mansion yielded $207 million in cash. The mansion belonged to alleged drug trafficker Zhenli Ye Gon, a Chinese-Mexican businessman known for gambling millions in Las Vegas casinos.

Police tracked Ye Gon to Maryland and arrested him there. He was accused of importing pseudoephedrine, a chemical used to make methamphetamine, from China and selling it on the Mexican black market. In his defense, Ye Gon's lawyers argued that the chemicals were intended for use in a cold-medicine factory. Ye Gon also claimed that $150 million of the money was not his, but it was part of an illegal campaign fund that crooked Mexican politicians forced him to guard.

Though Ye Gon remained in a US prison for two years, the case was dismissed in 2009 because one witness recanted and another refused to testify. Authorities suspect they were threatened, but there is no proof. Ye Gon remains in custody on immigration charges. He is currently fighting extradition to Mexico, where he would face charges of drug trafficking and tax evasion.

A RECESSION

President Calderón believes that one way to counter a military-trained force such as los Zetas is with the army. Now armored vehicles rumble through cities, and black-masked soldiers stop people on the streets to question them. Soldiers are masked for their own safety. If traffickers discover a soldier's identity, assassins could gun down him or his family.

Calderón's critics complain that his crackdown has no real effect on the drug trade and only pushes traffickers out of one place and into another.

Pro-Cartel Demonstrations

In February 2009, the Gulf cartel paid citizens in Monterrey to demonstrate against the presence of the army. Demonstrators often hide their faces, leading to the local name for them: *tapados*, or "covered ones." Cartels offer each *tapado* 200 pesos (approximately US$13) and a cell phone, or 500 pesos (US$33) and a backpack filled with school supplies.

The crackdown has not run drug traffickers out of Mexico, but it has only forced them to lie low and avoid drawing attention to themselves. Most citizens are not happy about the cartels, but the *narcos* do support the local economies with their purchases of private planes, luxury cars, and yachts. The drug lords still have plenty of money, but business in luxury brands is slow. "No one wants to be ostentatious right now," said Raúl Gustavo Piña Ibarra, manager of an idle Hummer and Cadillac

Los Zetas founder Flavio Méndez Santiago in Mexico City on January 18, 2011

dealership in the city of Culiacán.[8] This hurts businesses that rely on wealthy customers, many of whom are related to the drug cartels. Even banks are feeling the pinch. Instead of depositing their money, paranoid drug dealers hide it.

TRAFFICKERS PUSH BACK

September 15 is Independence Day in Mexico, and on that day in 2008, the streets in the city of Morelia were full of people celebrating. A husky man wearing black clothing approached and tossed a grenade into the crowd. Witnesses heard him beg forgiveness before he disappeared. Simultaneously, another man a few blocks away threw his own grenade and slipped away.

For a few seconds, people in the crowd thought the explosions were fireworks. Then the panic spread. Seven people were dead, and an eighth, a 13-year-old boy, would die later in the hospital. The attack wounded 106 people, including many children.

Authorities believed the attacks were intended to turn public opinion against President Calderón's crackdown, and they suspected that the la Familia cartel was responsible. In the following days, the la Familia cartel hung a banner reading, "Don't let them fool you: La Familia of Michoacán is with you and does not agree with acts of genocide."[9] In late September 2008, three members of los Zetas were arrested in connection with the attacks. The incident highlighted tensions between the government crackdowns, the cartels, and the common citizens who live in the areas where drug-related turf wars rage. ⌒

Bodies of migrants murdered by los Zetas in 2010

Hospital personnel attended a candlelight protest in memory of a Ciudad Juárez doctor who was kidnapped and killed in 2010.

KIDNAPPINGS

Mexico has been called "the kidnapping capital of the world."[1] The number of kidnappings in the country is difficult to determine because most citizens do not report the crimes. Although no one knows for sure, experts estimate that only one in ten kidnappings are reported. Victims' families often choose to handle kidnappings privately because of their distrust of police. Police corruption is rampant, and uniformed police officers—real or impersonators—sometimes capture victims.

Money and Power

Kidnapping is done for a few reasons, but kidnappers are usually financially motivated. Even successful drug cartels use kidnapping as a means to earn extra money, and specialized kidnapping rings have turned the practice into an industry. Also, kidnappers have gone after high-profile victims, including Mexican mayors and prominent businessmen. The kidnappers demonstrate that they have the power to get close to even the best-protected people. This creates a culture of fear in local communities. An upper-middle-class Mexican woman who wished to remain anonymous said,

> We cannot live under this pressure. All the time we are looking over our shoulder, the car windows always up, ringing the children on the cell at all times, having special passwords and codes in case, God forbid, of "trouble." This is not a life.[2]

Mayor of Santiago Kidnapped

Edelmiro Cavazos was the mayor of Santiago, an affluent town in the northern state of Nuevo León. He had a reputation as a kind man who helped his community. On the evening of August 15, 2010, gunmen abducted him from his home. A few days later, the mayor was found bound and blindfolded. He was dead.

Three main types of kidnappings happen in Mexico today. The conventional form of kidnapping—the abduction and ransom of a wealthy individual—is still common. However, middle-class and even poor people are now being targeted as well, though for much lower ransoms. Kidnappers may ask for only $500 to return a poor person to his or her family. However, payment of a ransom is no guarantee that an abducted person will be released alive.

A second type of kidnapping is called express kidnapping, because the ordeal usually takes only a few hours. During an express kidnapping, captors grab a victim and force him or her to withdraw money from ATMs. This sort of kidnapping requires only a few gang members, because the victim does not need to be housed or guarded for very long. More elaborate kidnappings require the involvement of many people.

The last kind of kidnapping is referred to as virtual kidnapping, because a captive is never actually taken. Instead, criminals call a home and pretend to have taken one of the family members. They demand a ransom and hope it is paid before the deception is discovered.

THE ABDUCTION OF FERNANDO MARTÍ

Wealthy businessman Alejandro Martí knew that his family presented a tempting target for kidnappers, so he did everything he could to keep them safe. His 14-year-old son, Fernando, was chauffeured to a private school in a bulletproof BMW sedan. He was also accompanied by his own bodyguard. On the morning of June 4, 2008, the sedan was stopped at a bogus police checkpoint. The driver saw what looked like real police officers, and he was right. The kidnappers were federal police, operating with criminal associates in a gang called *la Banda de la Flor* (the Flower Gang).

Fernando and his chauffeur were abducted, and the chauffeur was later killed. Cristián Salmones, the bodyguard, was strangled and left for dead.

Virtual Kidnapping Tactics

In many cases of virtual kidnapping, the victim picks up the phone to hear a screaming or pleading voice—a person pretending to be a child in danger. Thinking it is their own child, victims call out their child's name, giving the kidnapper this important information. From there, the kidnapper can manipulate the victim and demand money, jewelry, or other valuable items to be delivered before the victim finds out it is all a ruse.

The gang left their calling card—a single marigold—at the scene. The Martí family learned of the kidnapping when they received a phone call demanding a huge ransom. They did not call the police, but hired a private negotiating service instead. "Those who grabbed him were police officers, and the last thing we wanted was for the police to be involved," Alejandro Martí explained.[3]

After a brief negotiation, the full ransom was left in a parked car, as the kidnappers demanded. Then all communication ceased. The Martí family worried until, on August 1, Fernando's body was discovered in the trunk of a car along with a wilted marigold. He had been dead for weeks. A note with the body read, "For not paying. Yours Truly, *La Familia*."[4]

This was mystifying; after all, the family had paid the ransom. Investigators later learned that the note was a lie, and la Familia was not involved. Although newspapers initially reported that Salmones had died, the bodyguard recovered and was able to identify the kidnappers.

Five people were arrested, including Sergio Ortiz Juárez, a former police investigator. Numerous other police officers are under investigation. Investigators also believed that some of the gang

Alejandro Martí built a successful chain of sporting goods stores. His son was kidnapped and murdered in 2008.

members posed as members of an upper-class family. "They passed themselves off as a wealthy family to be able to get into the highest social circles to establish friendships, ties and relationships with people," said Mexico City Prosecutor Miguel Ángel Mancera.[5]

An Express Kidnapping

Julián Hakim was a medical student living on a shoestring budget in Mexico City. He did not have much money, so he never thought he was at risk for kidnapping. In 2010, he was making his way across a parking garage, heading for his beat-up Volkswagen.

Two men suddenly flanked him, pressing guns into his body. "You guys can take the car, just let me get out," Hakim told them. "I don't know why you need me. Take the car, take my wallet."[6]

The men forced Hakim into his car and drove him to an ATM, where they made him withdraw the maximum daily limit of

Protective Services Are Booming

Personal protection is a growing industry in Mexico. Numerous companies offer kidnap prevention, firearms training, and home security services. Nervous business executives are hiring bodyguards and paying to have their cars bulletproofed. Mansions and even middle-class homes are being fortified with armored doors, closed-circuit television surveillance, and electronic security systems.

For a while, wealthy people were even having microchips implanted into their bodies so their locations could constantly be beamed to satellites. This practice has declined since professional kidnapping rings have acquired scanners to locate the chips. Once abductors find one they cut it out with a knife.

If a kidnapping occurs, security companies have crisis response teams that send experienced hostage negotiators to the scene. Hostage negotiating can be a risky profession. In 2008, hostage negotiator Félix Batista was kidnapped in Mexico after giving a speech on kidnap prevention. No ransom was demanded, so the incident appears to have been a warning from gangsters to anyone who resists them.

cash from his credit cards. Then Hakim's captors drove around the city aimlessly, amusing themselves by beating him. Hakim later said,

> *Anything I said, I'd get hit. I'd get hit in the ribs. Or I'd get hit in the face. Anything. They'd be like, "Why you talking back?" Boom! And they'd hit me.* [7]

Almost six hours later, the kidnappers left Mexico City and headed north, still beating Hakim with their guns. Hakim said,

> *It got to a point where it was very painful, but mentally I was torn into pieces. I was just so scared for my life. I didn't care if they left the biggest bruise in the world; I just didn't want them to kill me. The mental scars they left on me were the worst.* [8]

After warning Hakim that if he called the police they would kill him, the kidnappers finally threw him out of the car. Hakim later did make a police report, but as is common

Will Loosening Gun Laws Help?

Mexico's strict gun laws make it difficult for ordinary citizens to legally acquire firearms. With the exception of government employees, Mexican citizens wanting handguns must be able to prove need in order to carry one. They are also required to post a bond—a fee in case of damages—and provide five character references. Some suggest relaxing these laws so that citizens can carry guns to protect themselves and dissuade kidnappers. These pro-gun supporters echo an argument familiar in pro-gun factions in the United States: where guns are outlawed, only outlaws will have guns.

The Death Penalty for Kidnappers

There is currently no death penalty in Mexico, but it may become law someday. Polls show that 75 percent of citizens feel the death penalty is appropriate for kidnappers who kill their victims. "These are people who won't be rehabilitated in jail," said Humberto Moreira, governor of Coahuila, a state bordering Texas. "Let's get real and let's start executing the kidnappers."[9]

in Mexico, his attackers were never arrested. Hakim's story, along with the abduction in the Martí family and countless others, highlight issues of police corruption that are frighteningly widespread.

During raids in Tijuana homes, law enforcement officers have found kidnapping victims held inside cages.

Police officer Jesús Martínez, center, was arrested in 2007. Martínez was suspected of working for the Arellano Félix cartel.

CORRUPTION

*I*n many places throughout Mexico,
corruption is engrained in the culture.
It is common to pay small bribes to get phone
service and garbage collection. Larger bribes are
required when applying for bank loans or building

permits. Mexican traffic police are perhaps the most notorious extortionists of all. A favorite ploy is to pull over drivers and threaten them with trumped-up charges and fines. Most drivers understand that they can pay their "fines" on the spot, in cash. This form of extortion is so common that it has a name: *la mordida*, meaning "the bite."

Considering this, it is not surprising that a higher-stakes version is played out among drug traffickers, politicians, and police. "The cartels have become so infiltrated in government that they're always two steps ahead," said T. J. Bonner, president of the National Border Patrol Council. "You have a culture of corruption in Mexico, which is part of the problem."[1]

POLICE TAKE SIDES

Various factions of police may be paid off by one cartel or another, and when cartels battle, police can get involved. This happened in September 2008, when federal police in Coahuila apprehended seven drug traffickers. The Coahuila police were attacked on the highway

Cops Demand Bribe from US State Senator

In October 2009, Senator Michelle Fischbach of Minnesota was driving in Cancún, Mexico. Police pulled her over and demanded a bribe. They wanted between $200 and $300 to let her go. The senator filed an extortion complaint, and now those officers are under investigation.

INCINERACION DE DROGA

Mexican army and federal forces incinerated seized drugs in Tijuana in 2009.

by police officers from Torreón, who attempted to free the suspects. A shootout occurred between the two factions of police, and the men from Coahuila won. In the end they killed one corrupt officer, wounded one more, and took 33 prisoners.

The event underscores the difficulty President Calderón is having in rooting out corruption in the police force. His solution has been to bring in the military, but military officers are not immune to corruption either. In 1997, Army General José de Jesús Gutiérrez Rebollo was arrested for taking payoffs from the Juárez cartel. At the time, he was Mexico's top antidrug official. And in 2009, Mexican Marines coordinated with US intelligence to carry out an assault on Arturo Beltrán Leyva, a cartel leader known for paying off Mexican officials.

WARDEN ALLOWED INMATES OUT OF PRISON

In another display of corruption, the warden of Gómez Palacio prison in Durango allowed inmates to be released at night to commit murders. The inmates were supplied with guns borrowed from guards and were transported in police cars. After the hits were carried out, the prisoners were then returned to their cells. The inmates are believed to be responsible for a July 18, 2010, attack on a birthday party that left 17 people dead. The guns they used were later linked to two other massacres that occurred the same year.

In a video that circulated on the Internet, two masked men believed to be members of los Zetas interrogated police officer Rodolfo Majera, who was kneeling on the

Inmates Walk Out of Jail

On December 17, 2010, 141 inmates strolled out of a jail in Nuevo Laredo near the Texas border. "They left by the front door, which points to complicity of the prison guards," said a police source who refused to be identified.[2] The prison's director and 44 guards were arrested after the escape.

ground between them. Majera admitted that he received payoffs from a drug lord, and confirmed that the 17 murders took place with the approval of the warden. The video ended with Majera's execution. Although a confession at gunpoint did not constitute proper evidence, it was one piece of the puzzle. On July 25, 2010, Warden Margarita Rojas Rodríguez, her deputy, and two security chiefs were arrested. Ricardo Najera, a spokesman for Mexico's Interior Ministry, said,

Secret Diplomatic Cables Leaked

"The Calderon Administration's courage, initiative and success have exceeded all expectations," said *The International Narcotics Control Strategy Report,* a US government publication.[3] However, the WikiLeaks Web site released secret documents with a much different message in 2010. Two classified documents from the US Embassy in Mexico revealed that the situation there is more serious than the US government let on. The cables contain statements by Mexican officials expressing concern that the government is losing some of its territory to the cartels, which now essentially rule some regions. The officials confided that time was "running out" to gain control over drug-related bloodshed.[4]

In one document, diplomat John D. Feeley of the US Embassy in Mexico summed up the Mexican political situation.

Official corruption is widespread, leading to a compartmentalized siege mentality among "clean" law enforcement leaders and their lieutenants. Prosecution rates for organized crime-related offenses are dismal; 2% of those detained are brought to trial.[5]

The communication concluded that Calderón's approval ratings were dropping as a result of his failing battle with the cartels.

The delinquents were committing their executions as part of a debt-settling scheme against members of rivaling groups from organized crime. Unfortunately, in these executions, these delinquents also cowardly murdered innocent civilians.[6]

DRUG CZAR ARRESTED

In November 2009, Mexico's highest-ranking antidrug official was arrested for taking bribes from the Sinaloa cartel. The drug czar, federal prosecutor Noé Ramírez Mandujano, headed the organized crime investigation office known as SIEDO. The arrest was made as a result of investigations conducted in connection with *Operación Limpieza* (Operation Cleanup), President Calderón's anticorruption initiative.

Mandujano apparently met regularly with cartel members while he was in office. He is accused of accepting $450,000 a month for tipping off cartel members about investigations and actions against them.

Coordinated Attacks in Guadalajara

Cartel commandos launched seven attacks on February 1, 2011, across the city of Guadalajara. Attackers blocked streets by burning commuter trains and a bus and throwing grenades at a police station. "This is an orchestrated attack by criminal forces," said Fernando Guzmán Pérez, interior secretary of the state of Jalisco. "There have been arrests . . . of people linked to these cells of organized crime, and perhaps it was because of those detentions that attacks over the past few hours broke out."[7]

CLEANING UP CORRUPTION

In August 2010, 3,200 Mexican police officers were fired as part of a corruption cleanup effort. That number represented almost 10 percent of Mexico's police force. More than 1,000 others faced disciplinary measures for failing screening tests.

The Mexican government is aware that some police corruption problems can be traced back to low salaries. Poorly paid workers could be tempted to take extra money in the form of bribes. The majority of officers only have grade school educations, and if they are fired, they have few job prospects outside the cartels. Calderón is addressing the corruption problem by increasing police salaries, and he is working toward a requirement for officers to have college degrees. In a nationwide address, the Mexican president asked that his citizens stand together against the cartels. "This is a battle that is worth fighting because our future is at stake," he said. "It's a battle that, with all Mexicans united, we will win."[8] The effort to clean up the police was widely celebrated, but cynics point out that many other purges of police departments have occurred over the years without lasting results.

In 2008, soldiers performed a training exercise to combat drug smuggling in Mexico City.

Cartel boss Edgar Valdéz Villarreal was arrested at this mansion in 2010. Some adolescents idolize drug lords for their lavish lifestyles.

How the Drug War Affects Youth

A small wooden cross is stuck in the dirt to mark the spot where 19-year-old Felipe Alejandro Prado and two other teenagers were killed. Felipe was chatting with his 14-year-old cousins on the curb outside their Tijuana home when the gunmen attacked. Exactly why the teens were shot is unclear, but the dispute was probably related to Felipe's job as a small-time drug peddler. As Felipe's nine-year-old brother, Arturo, peered into the coffin, an 11-year-old friend remarked, "When I grow up I want to be a narco, and get all the women and the money."[1]

Rumors of a Child Assassin

In Mexico, rumors circulated about a child assassin said to be about 12 years old. A YouTube video posted in November 2009 provided the first clue that the rumors were true. The video showed teenage Mexican boys posing with guns and dead bodies. One boy claimed to be an accomplice of the young killer known as *el Ponchis*, and boasted that they made $3,000 per murder. "When we don't find the rivals, we kill innocent people, maybe a construction worker or a taxi driver," the boy said.[2]

Some of the youths shown on the video were later arrested, and

Narcocorridos

Narcocorridos are ballads that celebrate the exploits of narcotraffickers. The Mexican government disapproves of the ballads because they glamorize the drug trade, making traffickers out to be macho and heroic. Individual drug lords often commission songs from musicians in order to boost their own fame. Musicians who sing *narcocorridos* about one trafficker are blacklisted by their patron's rivals, and more than a few singers have ended up dead.

authorities discovered that they worked for the South Pacific cartel (SPC). The SPC is a faction of the fragmented Beltrán Leyva cartel, led by Hector Beltrán Leyva. Former members have been battling for control of the cartel since Mexican Marines killed its original leader, Arturo Beltrán Leyva, in 2009. Authorities estimate that the SPC committed 200 murders in 2010 alone.

Such infighting was once dismissed by authorities, who viewed cartel violence as a problem that resolved itself. Cartel wars were mockingly called "self-cleaning ovens," a term police have used for other gang conflicts. This has not happened in Mexico because drug profits tempt in new players as fast as people are killed. Now authorities understand that infighting between cartels affects the wider world. Innocent citizens may be caught

Teaching Survival in School

Lillian Díaz, a Ciudad Juárez schoolteacher, teaches her class of 12-year-olds more than just academics. She coaches them on how to survive. "What do you do when you hear gunfire?" she prompts. "We lie on the floor!" the children chorus back.[3] The teacher asks who has witnessed a killing, and almost every hand in the room goes up. Díaz talks frankly about the cartel killings and dismemberments that are going on in broad daylight. "Look away if you see this happening," she advises. "Otherwise you could also be shot."[4]

in the crossfire between battling gangs, or their children may be recruited as cannon fodder. With fortunes at stake, wars between cartels spread until entire communities are caught up in the violence.

Fourteen-Year-Old Assassin Arrested

On December 3, 2010, Mexican soldiers surrounded a skinny, curly haired kid and herded him in front of a crowd of reporters. The boy looked tiny next to the burly men in their black masks and bulletproof vests. But this was a big bust; the police had arrested Edgar Jiménez Lugo, the child assassin known as *el Ponchis*. The boy was calm as he told reporters how the SPC had abducted him. Edgar said,

> When I was 11, they picked me up. They said they would kill me . . . I've killed four people, decapitated them. I felt bad doing it. They made me. They said if I didn't do it, they would kill me.[5]

Videos on the boy's cell phone confirmed that he had indeed joined the cartel. One showed Edgar holding a Kalashnikov rifle and posing at the front of a group of armed men. Another showed him using a stick to beat a man who was hanging by his arms.

Child assassin el Ponchis *was captured in 2010.*

The police arrested Edgar and his two sisters, 19-year-old Elizabeth Jiménez Lugo and 23-year-old Lina Erika Jiménez, on their way to an airport near Cuernavaca. Edgar and Elizabeth were preparing to flee the country, and Lina was driving them to the airport. Judging from the dirty clothes they had crammed into their bags, the pair had left in a hurry. They were carrying two plane tickets to Tijuana, along with guns and a few packages of cocaine. The plan was to sneak into the United States and join their mother, who had been living there illegally for years.

Elizabeth told police she was the girlfriend of a cartel boss called Julio Padilla, or *el Negro*. She admitted working for the SPC with a group of girls who disposed of the bodies of victims, but she wanted to start a new life. "These kids are victimizers, but they are also victims," said Miguel Barrera, a reformed gang member who now works to rehabilitate violent teenagers.[6]

A COCAINE BABY

How does a child grow into a killer? For Edgar, the process began before he was born. Routine testing in the San Diego hospital where his mother gave birth revealed traces of the cocaine his mother, Yolanda Jiménez Lugo, took during her pregnancy. She immediately lost custody, and the infant Edgar and his five siblings went into foster care.

The children eventually were sent to live with their grandmother in Cuernavaca, Mexico. Shortly after that, Edgar's father, David Jiménez, returned to Mexico, where he lived in the same compound as his young son. While Edgar's grandmother, Doña Carmen, was alive, she cared for the children. After she died, Edgar was forgotten, and he dropped out of school after the third grade. "I neglected him a little," admitted David Jiménez.[7]

RECRUITING ORPHANS

More than 1,100 children have died in the drug war since the beginning of Calderón's

Wives and Children

The wives and children of cartel bosses live in luxury, but they also live in fear. Families of drug lords are always in danger from rival cartels. "They are revenge killings. They settle scores. One way to hurt a rival is to kill the woman he loves most," said Ricardo Ravelo of the Mexican news magazine *Proceso*.[8]

One famous killing occurred in the 1990s, when Héctor Palma, known as *el Guero,* and his partner Joaquín Guzmán Loera, known as *el Chapo,* were battling the Arellano Félix cartel for control of the border crossing at Mexicali. *El Guero* had a famously beautiful wife named Guadalupe Leija. When a handsome Venezuelan named Rafael Clavel seduced her, she took her two young children and went with him willingly to San Francisco.

Guadalupe did not know that Clavel was working for the Arellano Félix cartel, and the entire romance was a farce. He killed her there in San Francisco and mailed her head back to her husband. Clavel then took her children to Venezuela, where he murdered them by throwing them off a bridge. Clavel was imprisoned in Venezuela, where he, too, was killed.

2006 crackdown on the cartels.
About 50,000 more have lost one
or both parents in the violence. In
border towns, wages are so low that
widows have to work two factory
shifts just to support their families.
Meanwhile, their children roam the
streets unsupervised, becoming easy
recruits for traffickers. There are
300 murders a month in Ciudad
Juárez alone, so cartels always need
replacements.

Perhaps it is a measure of the
carnage that cartels are recruiting
younger and younger kids. They
start by paying street kids to act as
lookouts or delivery boys. Orphaned
boys are eager to get attention from
father figures and to have a feeling of
belonging. But soon those boys and
some girls are committing crimes
themselves. What will become of these
children when they grow up? "There
is an enormous cost because these
kids aren't children as they should

The Hazards of Beauty

Narcotraffickers often
select beautiful teenage
girls and take them as
mistresses. Some families
are delighted when a drug
lord comes courting, but
others are terrified. Their
daughter might become
one of the *narco*'s many
mistresses, locked in
one of his houses. If the
couple breaks off their
relationship, the girl
becomes untouchable in
the community. No one
would dare date her for
fear of offending a powerful man.

be," says Irma Casas, who runs a women's shelter in Ciudad Juárez. "They are future criminals. What other aspirations are they going to have? What kind of future awaits them?"[9] There are many questions about the future of these children—and about the future of Mexico as the drug war rages on.

*In Ciudad Juárez, Mexican children turned in toy guns during
a program intended to combat violence in the city.*

US Secretary of State Hillary Clinton visited Mexico in March 2010 to discuss cartel violence on both sides of the border.

THE MEXICAN DRUG WAR
AND THE UNITED STATES

The United States shares some involvement in—and some of the blame for—the Mexican drug war because the US demand for drugs keeps Mexican drug cartels in business. Some drugs are sold in Mexico, but cartels make the majority of their profits by transporting drugs across the border. During a 2009 visit to Mexico, US Secretary of State Hillary Clinton said, "Our insatiable demand for illegal drugs fuels the drug trade."[1]

US Demand for Drugs

In 2011, the Reuters news service reported that the United States was the main destination for illegal drugs in the world. Other sources note that the United States has the highest rate of illegal drug use in the world, despite strict laws against these substances. Of these illegal substances, numbers of users of marijuana, cocaine, methamphetamine, and heroin remain high—and the demographic for many of these substances is getting younger. For example, heroin use tends to be cyclical. It makes an appearance, usage increases, and then eventually declines. However, in the next generation, heroin makes a comeback among naive young users who do not always know the risks associated with use,

Catapulted across the Border

Many drugs are smuggled across the border in hidden compartments in cars or on a person's body. But smugglers are finding new ways to transport drugs. In early 2011, National Guard members watching surveillance footage saw people catapulting packages of marijuana over the border to the United States. Mexican authorities were alerted, and the catapult was seized. It was capable of launching 4.4 pounds (2 kg) at a time. The people operating the catapult fled before they could be captured.

which include addiction, possible death from overdose, and the risk of contracting diseases from shared needles. Authorities are concerned that such a resurgence in heroin use among youth may be occurring now. In 2008, Dr. Carlos Tirado, a psychiatry professor at UT Southwestern Medical Center and medical director of a drug treatment center in Dallas, said,

> *Reports that we were seeing were pretty striking. Kids as young as 9 or 10 years of age coming to the hospital emergency rooms or detox facilities in acute heroin withdrawal.* [2]

The increase in heroin use among kids is no accident; it is part of a calculated marketing plan by Mexican and Colombian drug traffickers. Some heroin packages are decorated with images from popular films such as *Twilight*. Others carry brand names such as Chevrolet or Prada, even

Shared Needles Transmit Disease

Intravenous drug users are those who take drugs by injecting them. Injectable drugs include heroin and cocaine. These users are at high risk for contracting and spreading lethal diseases such as the human immuno-deficiency virus (HIV) and hepatitis C. HIV is the virus that causes acquired immunodeficiency syndrome (AIDS), and hepatitis C infects the liver. Both of these diseases can also be contracted by having unprotected sex with an infected person. Drugs increase impulsivity and remove inhibitions, making unsafe sex more likely among users. Both HIV and hepatitis C are more common among intravenous drug abusers than they are in the general population.

though those companies have nothing to do with drugs. "Those drug traffickers were marketing that heroin directly towards teenagers," says John Gilbride of the Drug Enforcement Administration (DEA) in New York.[3]

Many of these drugs are extremely addictive. This addiction keeps users hungry for more of the product, which keeps drug cartels profitable. For example, the coca plant is grown in Colombia, Peru, and Bolivia. Coca is refined into cocaine, which is smuggled across the US–Mexico border. Users snort, smoke, or inject refined cocaine for its "high." Although a euphoric, excited state is desired, users may also become paranoid, agitated, or violent. Users feel depressed and exhausted when the drug wears off and experience desperate cravings for more cocaine.

In Colombia, it is cheap to grow coca bushes and process the leaves into cocaine. Because there is high

Drug Addiction

Survival-oriented activities, such as eating, trigger pleasure responses from reward centers in the brain. Addictive drugs trigger these reward centers too. In psychological addiction, an addict is dependent on the "high" feeling produced by the drug.

Long-term drug use can also cause physical addiction, in which a tolerance to the mind-altering properties of the drug develops. When a person stops using a drug, he or she might go through withdrawal. Withdrawal symptoms include nausea, tremors, and sweating. Sudden withdrawal from certain substances can be risky, so medical supervision is important.

risk in smuggling the cocaine, each trafficker can charge a risk premium because he or she might get caught and be sent to prison. From South America to US streets, a drug becomes more valuable each time it changes hands. The risk to the traffickers is the main reason why illegal drugs are expensive and it explains why traffickers are willing to kill over its profits.

US Firearms

In addition to providing a steady demand for illegal drugs, the United States also provides Mexican cartels with smuggled weapons. Guns are very difficult to purchase legally in Mexico, but smugglers move US weapons to cartels there. Between 2007 and 2009, nearly 70,000 guns were found in Mexico that originated in the United States. Assault rifles are the biggest threat to lightly armed Mexican police. Fully automatic assault rifles can be purchased legally from gun stores in Texas and Arizona and resold illegally in Mexico.

The ATF is a branch of US law enforcement within the Bureau of Alcohol, Tobacco, Firearms and Explosives. In 2006, the ATF began implementing Project Gunrunner with the specific intent to stop the flow of firearms being smuggled into Mexico for use by gangs and cartels. According to the group, as of 2011, Project Gunrunner has aided in the recovery of more than 10,000 firearms intended for Mexico.

However, a report issued in late 2010 by the US Justice Department criticized the program for not sharing information with law enforcement partners in Mexico and the United States, thus weakening the potential for far-reaching effectiveness. Additionally, in early 2011, a secret ATF program called "Fast and

Decreased Tourism

Another way in which US citizens influence what happens in Mexico is through tourism. Acapulco, Cancún, Puerto Vallarta, and other cities on the Pacific Ocean or the Gulf of Mexico are popular tourist destinations for US travelers. These tourists stimulate local economies when they visit hotels, restaurants, and other businesses. But drug-related violence has scared away some tourists, and businesses in Mexico are suffering.

For example, in early 2011, 15 men were decapitated and two police officers were killed in Acapulco. News of violent incidents such as this can intimidate people looking to plan a vacation. As a result, local businesses are negatively impacted as potential tourists travel elsewhere. Beaches and pools are barely visited. Nightclubs and restaurants seem almost deserted. Additionally, major cruise lines with stops in Mexican cities have rearranged their routes to avoid these ports. Humberto López, an Acapulco businessman who has seen a decrease in traffic in his city, urges tourists not to be scared. "It doesn't have anything to do with ordinary people. Nobody is going to come up and shoot you," he said.[4]

Dead bodies were found in Acapulco in January 2011. Acapulco's tourist industry has been affected by the drug violence there.

Furious" was exposed. In this program, ATF agents allowed guns into Mexico with the intention of following them to see where they ended up. Mexican law enforcement agents were not told about this program, and many people spoke out against it, saying it was too dangerous and risky. The program continues to be controversial.

Opinions differ about the best way for the United States to stop this dangerous smuggling that provides the drug cartels with destructive weapons that fuel the violence. The US government has committed millions of dollars to programs intended to fight the smuggling problem.

The Merida Initiative

In recognition of the United States' shared responsibility for the drug problem, US President George W. Bush signed the Merida Initiative in June 2008. The Merida Initiative is a three-year program that provides crime-fighting support to Mexico, Central America, Haiti, and the Dominican Republic. Mexico received $400 million the first year, mainly in the form of equipment such as aircraft and surveillance devices. Mexican police receive equipment and training under the

Providing Guns to Cartels

On January 24, 2011, 20 people were arrested in Arizona. They were accused of buying guns for the Sinaloa cartel. This practice is known as "straw buying" because a person makes a purchase on behalf of someone else. The straw buyers passed background checks in which they claimed the guns were for personal use. Seven of the men spent $104,251 in cash for 140 guns, including AK-47 assault rifles. Another man bought as many as 20 AK-47s on each of several visits to the Lone Wolf Trading Company in Glendale, Arizona. Some of the weapons were found hidden in a television and a stove that were being transported into Mexico.

program, which also funds drug treatment and gang prevention programs. No weapons or cash were transferred as part of the agreement.

Another $300 million of aid was slated for the second year of the Merida Initiative. Additional funding brings the total cost of the program to $1.6 billion. The program will overhaul the Mexican judicial system and establish a method for tracking repeat offenders through the system. It also initiates a witness protection program for Mexican citizens threatened for testifying against cartels. The Merida Initiative continued into 2011 but shifted focus to emphasize police training.

In 2011, the United States seized a large group of weapons smugglers intended to bring into Mexico.

Traffickers who smuggle drugs across the border bring drug-related violence into the United States as well.

THE MEXICAN DRUG WAR ON US SOIL

The Mexican drug war has been a distant problem to many in the United States, who mostly only hear about it on the news. However, this is a problem that crosses borders. Cartels are moving into the United States and associating with US gangs who have the contacts to acquire weapons and distribute drugs.

CARTELS ALLIED WITH US GANGS

In prison, the white supremacist Aryan Brotherhood and the Hispanic-American gang called the Mexican Mafia are at violent odds against each other. Outside prison, the gangs cooperate. "They realize that the financial gain is so lucrative that they have been willing to work together," said Kevin O'Keefe, chief of the Bureau of Alcohol, Tobacco, Firearms and Explosives criminal intelligence division. "It's all about business."[1]

Members of the Aryan Brotherhood have a distinctive look that makes them easy to spot. In February 2010, some members of the all-white gang were arrested in a Hispanic area of Texas, trying to smuggle stolen cars to Mexican cartels. "It was pretty odd to see people like that in Brownsville," police lieutenant James Paschall said.

US Gangs Now Trafficking Humans

Alliances with Mexican cartels have allowed US gangs to branch out from their traditional pursuits of drug trafficking and weapons dealing and enter the business of human smuggling. These gang members agree to help traffic people illegally into the United States for a high fee. However, smugglers who are about to be caught sometimes abandon their human cargo, leaving them to die of thirst in the desert.

"They had the shaved heads, the tattoos, the whole bit. They stuck out like a sore thumb."[2]

Rogue Assassins in the United States

Jorge Rojas-López and his brother, Victor, were once enforcers for the Arellano Félix cartel, with Victor in command of their squad. Sometime around 2003, Victor was killed by his boss for insubordination when he refused an order to execute one of his men. Jorge took command of the squad, left the cartel, and escaped with his followers to San Diego. "They have killed my family and my brother," Jorge later said. "I had to do something, and I have the nerve to do it over here."[3]

He named his gang *los Palillos* (the Tooth-picks) after Victor, who was thin and strong. *Los Palillos* began drug trafficking and killing for hire, working from quiet suburban homes. They made millions but never forgot their vendetta against the Arellano Félix cartel. In 2004, they killed three Arellano Félix traffickers and stole a large load of marijuana. The cartel sent an assassin after Jorge, but *los Palillos* caught and killed the man before he could carry out the hit.

By 2007, the gang had expanded through the Midwest and into Florida, and the bodies of their rivals kept piling up. The rogue gang came to an end on June 16, 2007, when Jorge and another leader were arrested after kidnapping a high-level Arellano Félix drug trafficker.

MEXICAN DRUGS SOLD IN HIGH SCHOOLS

Colorado Springs, Colorado, is a conservative city known as the home of the Air Force Academy and Focus on the Family, a prominent Christian organization. It is also home to some very quiet Mexican cartel members. Colorado Springs is strategically located. It is ten hours north of the border town of Ciudad Juárez and right on the interstate highway system. That makes the city a major distribution point, where methamphetamine, cocaine, and heroin are hidden before they are divided up and sold. Highways that branch off east and west from this city are used to carry Mexican drugs into the US heartland.

The Mexican cartels have also sent dealers to sell their products on Colorado Springs streets. Daniel May, a district attorney in El Paso County, Colorado, said,

> We have had drugs flowing into our high schools. Unfortunately, in the last few years, we have seen heroin usage, in particular in a couple of our high schools, increasing. There's no question that it goes back to the Mexican cartels. And we have actually made arrests of—of Mexican cartel members directly supplying it to high school kids. [4]

So far, drug-related violence in the United States has not become the massive problem it is in Mexico. Drugs are being sold, but incidents of people being shot down on the streets

Mexican Heroin in Dallas Schools

Authorities suspect a prison gang called *Barrio Azteca* is importing heroin from Mexican cartels and selling it in the Dallas, Texas, area. A drug called "cheese," made of Mexican black tar heroin mixed with powdered over-the-counter cold pills, has been appearing in Dallas area high schools. This form of heroin is snorted rather than injected, a fact that makes it more appealing to young users who might be fearful of injections.

are rare. The reason is that shoot-outs are bad for business. El Paso County Sheriff Terry Maketa explained,

> *They don't want to send reckless individuals to be their front people in communities that are going to draw a lot of attention, because that goes against what they're here to do, and that is make money. And if they bring a lot of attention to themselves, if they bring about violence, not only is it going to affect the people they're hoping to sell to, but it's also going to capture the attention of law enforcement and bring the heat on them. And they know that.[5]*

BRINGING VIOLENCE TO US SOIL

However, isolated incidents of violence are creeping into the United States. In October 2010, a man was found beaten and decapitated in an apartment in Phoenix, Arizona. Investigators discovered that the victim had stolen a large

Mexican Cartels and the Mafia

In 2009, the DEA revealed that the Gulf cartel is moving cocaine across Texas to contacts in the Italian Mafia. "We've got some of the major cartel members established here dealing their wares in Europe," said James Capra, head of the US Drug Enforcement Administration's Dallas office.[6]

The drugs are transported across the Atlantic Ocean by New York associates of the Italian 'Ndrangheta criminal organization. Cocaine prices are about three times higher in Europe than in the United States because of the greater distance from South American coca fields.

The Santa Fe Bridge connects El Paso, Texas, top, with Ciudad Juárez, bottom. Close proximity to the United States makes Ciudad Juárez a hot spot for drug activity.

amount of marijuana from a powerful drug cartel. Decapitations are common in Mexican drug-related deaths, but they are rare on the US side of the border. Investigators believe that the gruesome murder was meant to send a message of warning.

As the effects of drug use and the violence related to the drug war become more apparent in the United

States, politicians and the public consider the best course of action to remedy the problems. From legalizing drug use to increasing government aid to Mexico, opinions on the best solutions vary widely.

California's state law enforcement displayed seized heroin and methamphetamine in 2010.

Tijuana doctors protested for peace in 2008.

No Easy Solutions

The problem of drug trafficking is a complicated one. Even the most ruthless cartels have their supporters among citizens, police, and politicians. Traffickers who get arrested or killed are quickly replaced by others willing to take the risks to reap the financial rewards. To make a bad situation worse, cartels throughout Mexico battle each other for territory, forcing citizens to live in a war zone. Drug users in the United States probably do not realize that their purchases contribute directly to the violence in Mexico. But many agree that US— and worldwide—demand for drugs creates a situation where violent drug cartels can thrive.

How can this problem be solved? Should penalties for possession be increased in order to cut demand? Should there be a crackdown on traffickers? Or, most controversial of all, should drugs be legalized so that criminal cartels are replaced by a well-regulated pharmaceutical industry?

PUNISHMENT OR EDUCATION

In the United States, the Controlled Substances Act determines penalties for drug offenses that vary based on the quantity and the relative danger of each drug. Drugs are divided into schedules I, II, III, IV, or V, with schedule I drugs being the most dangerous with no accepted medical applications. Schedule V drugs are prescription drugs with legitimate medical uses but some potential for abuse.

"Hard" and "Soft" Drugs

Some people categorize drugs as hard or soft. The distinction depends on the drug's perceived danger and potential for dependence, although many people believe the distinctions between hard and soft drugs are unclear and even misleading.

Heroin, methamphetamine, and cocaine are generally categorized as hard drugs with a high potential for health risk and addiction. Marijuana is often categorized as a soft drug along with alcohol and nicotine. However, soft drugs are not without risks. For example, users can become addicted to alcohol and nicotine, and marijuana has been associated with long-term health risks such as lung damage. Even so, supporters feel marijuana is less dangerous than alcohol, which is a socially accepted drug with numerous risks of its own.

Authorities agree that they want to reduce the demand for illegal drugs, but which is the better strategy: punishment or education? Penalties for drug trafficking are already severe. Traffickers caught with schedule I drugs such as heroin, cocaine, or LSD will receive mandatory jail time along with substantial fines. Penalties for repeat offenders are doubled. On a third offense, judges issue a mandatory life sentence.

The United States has the highest rate of incarceration in the world. In 2008, approximately 2.3 million people were in US jails. With a population four times the US population, China had only 1.6 million prisoners. Authorities are reluctant to make penalties harsher because US jails are overcrowded as they are. Critics point out that penalties do not seem to dissuade drug dealers, because even schedule I drugs are easy for users to find.

Those who are opposed to long prison terms for drug offenders suggest drug treatment programs as an alternative. However, not all patients who complete drug rehabilitation programs are cured, and relapse rates vary between 40 and 60 percent.

There does not seem to be any one strategy that prevents drug abuse entirely, although there are numerous tactics that reduce it. Studies have shown that drug prevention programs are effective at reducing drug use and cigarette smoking among young people. After-school programs and extracurricular activities also reduce drug use among participating students, as do random drug tests. Schools that enforce random drug testing programs do have lower rates of drug use among students, but only during the school year. Kids in the drug culture quickly learn how long they must stay off drugs during late summer to avoid testing positive in the fall. And some kids believe that more exotic drugs will not register on conventional drug tests, leading them to try dangerous substances.

THE PRO-LEGALIZATION ARGUMENT

Proponents of legalization believe that the war on drugs is more damaging to society than unregulated

drug use would be. They think that much of the
violence associated with drug trafficking arises simply
because drugs are illegal. Advocates of legalization
compare the modern war on drugs to alcohol
prohibition in the 1920s. During this time, a US
Constitutional amendment made the distribution
of alcohol illegal. During Prohibition, bootleggers
made fortunes brewing and selling alcohol, while
homicide rates skyrocketed.

Relatively few people support legalizing all
recreational drugs, but one of them is former Seattle
police chief Norm Stamper. Stamper is the author of
*Breaking Rank: A Top Cop's Exposé of the Dark Side of American
Policing*. Stamper said,

> The demand for illicit drugs is as strong as the nation's
> thirst for bootleg booze during Prohibition. It's a demand
> that simply will not dry up. . . . They're not about to stop,
> no matter what their government says or does. It's time to
> accept drug use as a right of adult Americans, treat drug
> abuse as a public-health problem and end the madness of
> an unwinnable war.[1]

Stamper envisions a drug regulation system
much like the system for alcohol, in which people
aged 21 and older have legal access to any and all

recreational drugs. In a legalized system, he argues, drugs could be produced at standard potencies, with pharmaceutical-level sanitation and purity. Additionally, drug prices would be lower because the drugs are cheap and easy to produce. A reduced price would remove the profit motive of illegal drug smuggling, cutting the financial incentive for cartels. In Stamper's view, legalization "would extract from today's drug dealing the obscene profits that attract the needy and the greedy and fuel armed violence."[2]

Some proponents of drug legalization—full or partial—have pointed out that enforcing current drug laws is expensive. Money is spent paying the salaries of law enforcement officers and judges, as well as paying for jail employees and facilities. Additionally, if drugs were legalized, they could be taxed

In Support of Legalization

A 2009 Gallup poll revealed that 44 percent of Americans support legalizing marijuana. Of those who consider themselves liberal, 78 percent are in favor of marijuana legalization, while only 28 percent of conservatives support the idea. Young people are more likely to support legalization than older people, suggesting that marijuana laws may change in the future.

at higher rates, like alcohol is. These financial motivations have been especially relevant because many states, as well as the federal government, are facing debt and budget cuts. Proponents of legalization believe that money saved and taxes earned could help alleviate these problems.

The DEA Opposes Legalization

The DEA disagrees. Its position is that illegal drugs are against the law because they are harmful. Instead of legalizing drugs, the DEA aims to stamp out their use with a combination of education, law enforcement, and drug treatment centers. Illicit drug use has declined by a third in the United States over the last 20 years, a statistic that supports the DEA's strategy.

Both pro-legalization and anti-legalization groups acknowledge that drugs and crime go hand-in-hand. But would legalization really reduce drug-related crime? The DEA thinks not. In a document entitled *Speaking Out Against Drug Legalization*, the agency argues that

> *Six times as many homicides are committed by people under the influence of drugs, as by those who are looking for money*

to buy drugs. Most drug crimes aren't committed by people trying to pay for drugs; they're committed by people on drugs.[3]

The majority of people in the debate side somewhere between the two polar extremes of legalization and prohibition. Prohibiting a substance that is illegal but thriving is impossible, critics say, and the idea of legalization has been skewed by public rhetoric that uses scare tactics to create a false concept of what legalization truly means. Even if laws do allow for legal

Will Medical Marijuana Cut Cartel Profits?

Marijuana remains illegal on the federal level, which complicates enforcement in states where medical marijuana is legal. As of 2011, 15 states plus the District of Columbia have enacted laws to legalize medical marijuana for patients with a doctor's recommendation. Supporters of legalized medical marijuana believe that many people suffering from chronic conditions would otherwise be buying from the cartels.

Before medical marijuana was legal in Arizona, a small number of patients bought marijuana at an underground dispensary called the Tucson Hemp Clinic. The proprietor, a 62-year-old who goes by the alias "Linda," bought eight pounds (3.6 kg) a month from a dealer supplied by Mexican cartels. In 2010, Arizona legalized medical marijuana for patients with conditions including chronic pain, cancer, and AIDS. Under the law, marijuana dispensaries will be required to grow their own marijuana. Linda's dealer was not happy when he learned she would no longer buy from him. He knocked her down and fired a shot at her, but he missed. Linda and other residents of this border state are hoping that Arizona dispensaries will drive off the drug cartels and lower the crime rate.

use of a drug, regulations could be specific to the drug at hand. For example, stricter laws could be in place for drugs deemed more dangerous.

WOULD LEGAL MARIJUANA SHUT DOWN THE CARTELS?

The number of people who support the legalization of marijuana is higher than the number of people who support the general legalization of drugs. Legalizing marijuana, supporters argue, would cut the profits of the Mexican cartels and replace those criminals with law-abiding businesspeople. But would legalizing marijuana really shut down the cartels? Stephen Gutwillig, the California director of the Drug Policy Alliance and a vocal supporter of marijuana legalization, said,

> Ending marijuana prohibition, bringing the multibillion-dollar marijuana market into the light of day and under the rule of law, will deal a major blow to criminal syndicates on both sides of the border.[4]

It is important to note that cartels still deal in cocaine, methamphetamine, and many other drugs, so legalizing marijuana would not put them out of business. If the legalization of marijuana has the potential to slash their profits, observers wonder what other illicit activity cartels would use to fill the gap.

On the other side of the marijuana debate, the DEA argues that marijuana is illegal for a reason. It is listed as a schedule I substance. Marijuana can cause short-term memory loss and affect judgment. Therefore, drivers who are under the influence of marijuana are a hazard. Opponents also worry that marijuana will become a gateway drug, meaning that users begin with it and then move on to abuse more dangerous substances.

In 2010, Californians rejected Proposition 19, which would have legalized marijuana in that state for people older than 21. But even though the proposition failed, 46.5 percent of voters voted in favor of legalization. Supporters of the ballot measure argued that legalization would devastate the Mexican cartels. The Rand Corporation, an independent research institute, determined that this was not true. Legalizing marijuana in the state of

Marinol

The synthetic drug dronabinol is derived from marijuana. It is marketed under the name Marinol. Doctors usually prescribed Marinol for cancer patients and those with HIV or AIDS. Like medical marijuana, Marinol controls nausea and vomiting and stimulates appetite. However, Marinol is taken in a pill form instead of through smoking. Possible side effects of the medication include nausea, vomiting, hallucinations, and dizziness.

In March 2011, Felipe Calderón and US President Barack Obama held a news conference in Washington DC. They discussed partnering to combat drug-related border violence.

California alone would cost the cartels only 2 to 4 percent of their profits. Proposition 19 could have had a significant impact on cartels if California marijuana were sold nationwide, but that is unlikely. "It's very hard to imagine that the feds would sit idly by and just let California marijuana dominate the country," said Beau Kilmer, codirector of Rand's Drug Policy Research Center.[5]

Prisons are already overcrowded and law enforcement is operating at its limit, so increased enforcement is unlikely. Legalization might shut down the cartels, but at what cost? Legalization could increase drug use and worsen the associated problems of addiction, child neglect, and irresponsibility.

Decreasing Demand and the Illusion of Happiness

US President Barack Obama and other White House officials have visited Mexico to meet with leaders there to discuss the problems surrounding the Mexican drug war. Citizens on both sides of the border have expressed their concerns to their respective governments, and these meetings are intended to increase communication between the two countries. To solve these problems, many believe the United States and Mexico need to partner with mutual goals instead of working independently.

On January 27, 2011, President Obama took questions from the public via YouTube. In answer to a question about suppressing crime by legalizing all drugs, the president said,

This is an entirely legitimate topic for debate. . . . I am not in favor of legalization. . . . When you think about other damaging activities in our society—smoking, drunk driving, making sure you're wearing seat belts—you know, typically we've made huge strides over the last 20, 30 years by changing people's attitudes. On drugs, I think that a lot of times we have been so focused on arrests, incarceration, interdiction that we don't spend as much time thinking about how do we shrink demand.[6]

Can society knock out the demand for drugs instead of just reducing it by a few percentage points? How can this be done? Certainly, education helps people understand the dangers of drugs, and rehabilitation helps them get sober. But some people still do things they know are risky. The problem is a complex and difficult one, because at its root is the quest for happiness. Drugs do not bring real happiness, but they create the temporary illusion of it. The drug problem is unlikely to go away, but families and groups of friends can take care of one another. Then perhaps fewer people will settle for an illusion. ⌐

A Central American migrant protested violence in Mexico in April 2011.

TIMELINE

1909

Legendary bandit Jesús Malverde is said to have been killed by police. He has become the patron saint of narcotraffickers.

1960s

With the help of Pedro Áviles, Miguel Ángel Félix Gallardo smuggles drugs into the United States from Sinaloa.

1970s–1980s

The toxic herbicide paraquat is sprayed on Mexican marijuana and opium poppy fields, but many contaminated plants were still sold.

1993

Powerful drug lord Pablo Escobar is shot dead by Colombian security forces in December.

circa 1995

After receiving training from US Army Special Forces, GAFE soldiers desert to become los Zetas.

2006

Members of la Familia roll five severed heads onto the dance floor of a Mexican disco.

1987	late 1980s	1989
Félix Gallardo moves his cartel to Guadalajara.	Félix Gallardo divides up his cartel.	Félix Gallardo is arrested for the torture and killing of a US federal agent.

2006	2007	2008
In December, Mexican President Felipe Calderón announces a crackdown on drug traffickers.	Police raid the home of alleged trafficker Zhenli Ye Gon and find $207 million in cash.	Teodoro García Simental and his followers engage in a shootout with the Arellano Félix cartel in April that leaves 15 dead.

TIMELINE

2008	2008	2008

Fourteen-year-old Fernando Martí is kidnapped on June 4. His dead body is found on August 1.

US President George W. Bush signs the Merida Initiative in June.

Los Zetas launch an Independence Day grenade attack on September 15.

2010	2010	2010

In July, a Mexican warden releases inmates to kill 17 people and then return to jail.

Los Zetas murder 72 migrants in August.

In August, 3,200 Mexican police officers are fired in a corruption cleanup effort.

2008

Arellano Félix cartel members are found murdered by rivals in August, September, and October.

2009

The Gulf cartel pays Monterrey citizens to demonstrate against the army in February.

2009

In November, Mexican drug czar Noé Ramírez Mandujano is arrested for taking bribes from the Sinaloa cartel.

2010

In October, a man is found beheaded in Phoenix, Arizona, in a drug-related incident.

2011

Los Zetas founder Flavio Méndez Santiago is arrested for human trafficking in January.

2011

Banners in Michoacán announce the dissolution of la Familia on January 25.

ESSENTIAL FACTS

AT ISSUE

❖ Cartels throughout Mexico can make good money through illegal drug trafficking. These groups battle each other for territory, forcing citizens to live in a war zone. Traffickers who are arrested or killed are quickly replaced by others willing to take risks for profit.

❖ Mexican drug cartels supply marijuana, heroin, cocaine, and methamphetamine to US users. Mexican drugs are smuggled north, and US guns are smuggled south to the private armies of the cartels.

❖ In poverty-stricken areas of Mexico, drug lords are often admired for their lavish lifestyles and for the community services they provide. Such acts of charity win *narcos* the support of locals, who help them evade capture. Some children are recruited to work for the cartels, and many people are willing to risk their lives to earn a profit rather than living a life of poverty.

❖ Cartels offer bribes and make threats to get authorities to look the other way. Even high-ranking officials are on cartel payrolls. Some law enforcement officers are involved in kidnappings, which have become common in the country. This creates a culture of distrust among law enforcement officers and citizens in Mexico.

❖ Recreational drugs are illegal because they carry health risks. Lethal overdoses, addiction, crime, and the destruction of relationships are some of the consequences of drug abuse. Some drugs trafficked through Mexico, including heroin, are being marketed to children in the United States. The Mexican cartels have also sent dealers to sell their products on US streets.

CRITICAL DATES

1960s
Miguel Ángel Félix Gallardo and Pedro Áviles trafficked drugs into the United States. Félix Gallardo eventually split up his cartel into

smaller groups. Throughout the years, the cartels grew and changed and new groups formed.

2006

In an effort to take a stand against the violence, Mexican President Felipe Calderón announced a crackdown on drug traffickers in December. The violence escalated, and the bodies of brutally murdered victims began to appear in public places.

2008

US President George W. Bush signed the Merida Initiative in June. The Merida Initiative is a three-year program that provides crime-fighting support to Mexico, Central America, Haiti, and the Dominican Republic.

2010

In August, 3,200 Mexican police officers were fired in a corruption cleanup effort. This action highlighted the widespread problem of corruption in Mexican law enforcement.

2011

A man was found beheaded in Phoenix, Arizona, in a drug-related incident. The incident proved that violence related to the Mexican drug war is moving into the United States.

Quotes

"Old cartels don't seem to go away; they just seem to morph into new variants over time. There's strong continuity for these organizations, dating back multiple generations of smugglers."
—David Shirk, director of the Trans-Border Institute at the University of San Diego

"The cartels have become so infiltrated in government that they're always two steps ahead. You have a culture of corruption in Mexico, which is part of the problem."—T. J. Bonner, president of the National Border Patrol Council

Essential Issues

GLOSSARY

abduction
A kidnapping.

assassin
A person who commits murder, often for payment.

cartel
In Mexico, a crime organization involved in drug trafficking; also called a drug-trafficking organization.

czar
An individual with a great deal of power or influence in a certain area.

eradicate
To wipe out or destroy utterly.

extortion
The practice of taking something by force or threat.

faction
A part of a larger group.

incarceration
Imprisonment.

indulgence
Something done or enjoyed as a special treat or pleasure.

inhibitions
Impulses that restrain or suppress behavior.

innovation
A new idea or method.

lucrative
Profitable.

Mafia
A criminal organization originating in Italy.

• 102 •

minions
> Servile followers or subordinates of a person in power.

ostentatious
> Describes a person who shows off wealth or ability in an attempt to impress others.

recant
> To publicly take back a statement; to renounce.

relegated
> Sent or consigned to an inferior position, place, or condition.

vendetta
> A bitter rivalry or feud with another person or group.

ADDITIONAL RESOURCES

SELECTED BIBLIOGRAPHY

Arsenault, Chris. "US-trained cartel terrorises Mexico." *Al Jazeera*. N.p., 3 Nov. 2010. Web.

Beith, Malcolm. *The Last Narco: Inside the Hunt for El Chapo, the World's Most-Wanted Drug Lord*. New York: Grove Press, 2010. Print.

Bowden, Charles. *Murder City: Ciudad Juárez and the Global Economy's New Killing Fields*. New York: Nation Books, 2010. Print.

"Mexico Under Siege." *Los Angeles Times*. N.p., 4 Mar. 2011. Web.

FURTHER READINGS

Gifford, Clive. *Gangs*. North Mankato, MN: Smart Apple Media, 2007. Print.

Hyde, Margaret O., and John F. Setaro. *Drugs 101: An Overview for Teens*. Brookfield, CT: Twenty-First Century Books, 2003. Print.

Lankford Jr., Ronald D., ed. *Organized Crime*. Greenhaven, 2009. Print.

Rooney, Anne. *How Should We Deal with Crime?* Mankato, MN: Arcturus, 2010. Print.

WEB LINKS

To learn more about the Mexican drug war, visit ABDO Publishing Company online at **www.abdopublishing.com**. Web sites about the Mexican drug war are featured on our Book Links page. These links are routinely monitored and updated to provide the most current information available.

For More Information

For more information on this subject, contact or visit the following
organizations:

Drug Abuse Resistance Education America (D.A.R.E.)
P.O. Box 512090, Los Angeles, CA 90051
800-223-DARE
www.dare.com
The D.A.R.E program consists of law enforcement officer–led
programs implemented in schools. The programs teach skills to
resist drugs, gangs, and violence. The program has expanded to
locations around the world.

InSight
4400 Massachusetts Avenue NW, Washington, DC 20016
202-657-6717
http://insightcrime.org
InSight studies organized crime in Latin America and the
Caribbean. The nonprofit organization has offices in Washington
DC and Colombia and offers a weekly online newsletter.

Washington Office on Latin America (WOLA)
1666 Connecticut Ave NW, Suite 400, Washington, DC 20009
202-797-2171
www.wola.org
WOLA focuses on the Latin American and Caribbean regions
and seeks to shape US policy regarding these global areas. WOLA
emphasizes human rights, democracy, and social justice through
partnerships with government and societal organizations.

SOURCE NOTES

Chapter 1. Drugs, Guns, and Money

1. Richard Marosi. "In Mexico, a police victory against smuggling brings deadly revenge." *Los Angeles Times*. N.p., 7 Sept. 2008. Web. 11 Feb. 2011.
2. Ibid.
3. Tracy Wilkinson. "Vatican suggests excommunicating Mexican drug traffickers." *Los Angeles Times*. N.p., 13 Jan. 2009. Web. 11 Feb. 2011.

Chapter 2. The History of the Cartels

1. Jake Bergman. "The Place Mexico's Drug Kingpins Call Home." *Frontline*. WGBH Educational Foundation, N.d. Web. 11 Feb. 2011.
2. Kate Murphy. "Mexican Robin Hood Figure Gains a Kind of Notoriety in U.S." *The New York Times*. The New York Times Company, 8 Feb. 2008. Web. 11 Feb. 2011.
3. "Nation: Panic over Paraquat." *Time*. Time Inc., 1 May 1978. Web. 11 Feb. 2011.
4. "Crime File—Famous Criminal: Pablo Escobar." *Crime & Investigation Network*. N.p., n. d. Web. 21 Mar. 2011.
5. Richard Marosi. "Tijuana killings may signal fall of Arellano Felix cartel." *Los Angeles Times*. N.p., 6 Oct. 2008. Web. 11 Feb. 2011.
6. Ibid.
7. Ibid.
8. Ibid.
9. Ibid.
10. Emily Schmall. "Drug King 'El Chapo' Is Mexico's Most Wanted." *AolNews*. AOLNews, 3 May 2010. Web. 11 Feb. 2011.

Chapter 3. The Crackdown

1. John Burnett. "Drugs Cross Border By Truck, Free Trade And Chance." *npr*. NPR, 8 Nov. 2010. Web. 19 Apr. 2011.
2. Kristen Bricker. "Mexico's Drug War Death Toll: 8,463 and Counting." *The Narcosphere*. N.p., 31 Dec. 2008. Web. 11 Feb. 2011.
3. Marc Lacey. "Grenade Attack in Mexico Breaks From Deadly Script." *The New York Times*. The New York Times Company, 24 Sept. 2008. Web. 11 Feb. 2011.
4. Kristen Bricker. "Mexico's Drug War Death Toll: 8,463 and Counting." *The Narcosphere*. N.p., 31 Dec. 2008. Web. 11 Feb. 2011.
5. Chris Arsenault. "US-trained cartel terrorises Mexico." *ALJAZEERA*. N.p., 3 Nov. 2010. Web. 11 Feb. 2011.
6. Michael Ware. "Los Zetas called Mexico's most dangerous drug cartel." *CNN*. Cable News Network, 6 Aug. 2009. Web. 11 Feb. 2011.
7. Chris Arsenault. "US-trained cartel terrorises Mexico." *ALJAZEERA*. N.p., 3 Nov. 2010. Web. 11 Feb. 2011.
8. Tracy Wilkinson. "Culiacan, Mexico, feels the pain of a drug-induced recession." *Los Angeles Times*. N.p., 21 Oct. 2008. Web. 11 Feb. 2011.
9. Marc Lacey. "Grenade Attack in Mexico Breaks From Deadly Script." *The New York Times*. The New York Times Company, 24 Sept. 2008. Web. 11 Feb. 2011.

Chapter 4. Kidnappings

1. Fred Burton and Scott Stewart. "Mexico: The Third War." *STRATFOR*. Stratfor Global Intelligence, 18 Feb. 2009. Web. 19 Apr. 2011.

2. Tim Padgett with Dolly Mascarenas. "In Mexico, a Kidnapping Negotiator Is Kidnapped." *Time*. Time Inc., 18 Dec. 2008. Web. 11 Feb. 2011.

3. Marc Lacey and Antonio Betancourt. "High-profile kidnapping stuns Mexico." *The Seattle Times*. The Seattle Times Company, 14 Aug. 2008. Web. 11 Feb. 2011.

4. Dolly Mascareñas. "No Help for Mexico's Kidnapping Surge." *Time*. Time Inc., 8 Aug. 2008. Web. 11 Feb. 2011.

5. Dudley Althaus. "5 jailed in kidnap-slaying of Mexican retailer's son." *chron*. The Houston Chronicle, 8 Sept. 2008. Web. 11 Feb. 2011.

6. Jason Beaubien. "Mexico's Drug War Spawns Wave Of Kidnappings." *NPR*. NPR, 26 Aug. 2010. Web. 11 Feb. 2011.

7. Ibid.

8. Ibid.

9. Marion Lloyd. "Mexico: Death Penalty Gaining Support." *The Huffington Post*. TheHuffingtonPost.com, Inc., 14 Jan. 2009. Web. 11 Feb. 2011.

Chapter 5. Corruption

1. "Calderon makes appeal as drug violence soars in Mexico." *The Washington Times*. The Washington Times, LLC, 16 June 2010. Web. 11 Feb. 2011.

2. Joshua Norman. "141 Prisoners Escape Mexico Border Jail." *CBSNews*. CBS Interactive Inc., 17 Dec. 2010. Web. 11 Feb. 2011.

3. Stephanie Hanson. "Mexico's Drug War." *Council on Foreign Relations*. Council on Foreign Relations, 20 Nov. 2008. Web. 11 Feb. 2011.

4. Tracy Wilkinson. "WikiLeaks cables reveal unease over Mexican drug war." *Los Angeles Times*. Los Angeles Times, 2 Dec. 2010. Web. 11 Feb. 2011.

5. Ibid.

6. CNN Wire Staff. "Mexican officials: Prison inmates released to commit killings." *CNN*. Cable News Network, 25 July 2010. Web. 11 Feb. 2011.

7. Arturo Pérez. "Gang gunbattles, street blockades in Mexico." *valleynewslive.com*. WorldNow and Valley News Live, 3 Feb. 2011. Web. 11 Feb. 2011.

8. "Calderon makes appeal as drug violence soars in Mexico." *The Washington Times*. The Washington Times, LLC, 16 June 2010. Web. 11 Feb. 2011.

Chapter 6. How the Drug War Affects Youth

1. "Tijuana Violence." *Los Angeles Times*. N.p., n.d. Web. 11 Feb. 2011.

2. Katherine Corcoran and Oswald Alonso. "14-year-old hit man." *Chicago Sun-Times*. Sun-Times Media, LLC, 5 Dec. 2010. Web. 11 Feb. 2011.

3. "Kids caught in Mexico's drug war." *ALJAZEERA*. N.p., 9 Apr. 2010. Web. 11 Feb. 2011.

4. Ibid.

5. Ioan Grillo. "In Teenage Killers, Mexico Confronts a Bloody Future." *Time*. Time Inc., 8 Dec. 2010. Web. 11 Feb. 2011.

SOURCE NOTES CONTINUED

6. Ken Ellingwood and Tracy Wilkinson. "Mexican drug cartels find youths to be easy prey." *Los Angeles Times*. Los Angeles Times, 18 Dec. 2010. Web. 11 Feb. 2011.

7. Ibid.

8. Catherine Bremer. "High-risk riches for Mexico's 'narco wives'." *Reuters*. Thomson Reuters, 27 Jan. 2009. Web. 11 Feb. 2011.

9. Catherine Bremer. "Special report: Mexico's growing legion of narco orphans." *Reuters*. Thomson Reuters, 6 Oct. 2010. Web. 11 Feb. 2011.

Chapter 7. The Mexican Drug War and the United States

1. Ken Ellingwood. "U.S. shares blame for Mexico drug violence, Clinton says." *Los Angeles Times*. N.p., 26 Mar. 2009. Web. 7 Mar. 2011.

2. John Burnett. "'Cheese' Heroin Hooking Young Users in Dallas." *NPR*. NPR, 26 Mar. 2008. Web. 11 Feb. 2011.

3. Sharyn Alfonsi and Hannah Siegel. "Heroin Use In Suburbs On The Rise." *ABC*. ABC News Internet Ventures, 29 Mar. 2010. Web. 11 Feb. 2011.

4. Ken Ellingwood. "Amid drug violence, Acapulco watches tourism recede." *The Seattle Times*. The Seattle Times Company, 18 Jan. 2011. Web. 7 Mar. 2011.

Chapter 8. The Mexican Drug War on US Soil

1. Kevin Johnson. "Drug cartels unite rival gangs to work for common bad." *USA Today*. USA TODAY, 16 Mar. 2010. Web. 11 Feb. 2011.

2. Ibid.

3. Solomon Moore. "How U.S. Became Stage for Mexican Drug Feud." *The New York Times*. The New York Times Company, 8 Dec. 2009. Web. 11 Feb. 2011.

4. "In Colorado, Authorities Battle Mexican Drug Cartels' Business Plans." *PBS NEWSHOUR*. MacNeil/Lehrer Productions, n.d. Web. 11 Feb. 2011.

5. Ibid.

6. McClatchy newspapers. "Mexican cartels funneling shipments to Italian mafia through Texas." *Guardian.co.uk*. Guardian News and Media Limited, 22 Apr. 2009. Web. 11 Feb. 2011.

Chapter 9. No Easy Solutions

1. Norm Stamper. "Legalize drugs—all of them." *The Seattle Times*. The Seattle Times Company, 4 Dec. 2005. Web. 11 Feb. 2011.

2. Ibid.

3. "Speaking Out Against Drug Legalization." *U.S. Drug Enforcement Administration*. N.p., n.d. Web. 11 Feb. 2011.

4. John Hoeffel. "Legalizing pot in California would hardly dent cartels' revenue, report says." *Los Angeles Times*. Los Angeles Times, 13 Oct. 2010. Web. 11 Feb. 2011.

5. Ibid.

6. Michael A. Memoli. "YouTube nation's burning question for Obama: What's his stand on marijuana legalization?" *Los Angeles Times*. N.p., 27 Jan. 2011. Web. 11 Feb. 2011.

INDEX

acquired immunodeficiency
  syndrome, 66, 89, 91
Aguiar Retes, Carlos, 12
Air Force Academy, 76
Airmobile Special Forces
  Group. *See* GAFE
al-Qaeda, 11
Alejandro Prado, Arturo, 55
Alejandro Prado, Felipe, 54–55
Ángel Mancera, Miguel, 41
Arellano Félix cartel, 21–23,
  60, 76
Aryan Brotherhood, 75
Áviles, Pedro, 18

Barrera, Miguel, 59
Barrio Azteca, 77
Batista, Félix, 42
Beltrán Leyva, Arturo, 49, 56
Beltrán Leyva, Hector, 56
Beltrán Leyva cartel, 56
Bonner, T. J., 47
Border Patrol, US, 7, 9, 13, 47
*Breaking Rank: A Top Cop's Exposé of
  the Dark Side of American Policing,*
  86
bribes, 8, 11, 19, 24, 30, 46,
  47, 51, 52
Bricker, Kristen, 31
Burnett, John, 27
Bush, George W., 71

Calderón, Felipe, 28, 32, 34,
  48, 50, 51, 52, 60
Camarena Salazar, Enrique, 21
Campbell, Howard, 24

Capra, James, 78
Carmen, Doña, 60
Casas, Irma, 62
Cavazos, Edelmiro, 38
Clavel, Rafael, 60
Clinton, Hillary, 65
cocaine, 10, 19, 59, 65, 66,
  67–68, 77, 78, 84, 90
Controlled Substances Act, 83
corruption in Mexico, 7, 8, 13,
  27, 37, 44, 46–52

Deare, Craig, 29
death penalty, 44
Díaz, Lillian, 56
drug addiction, 11, 12, 66, 67,
  84, 93
Drug Enforcement
  Administration, 30, 67, 78,
  88, 91
drug legalization, 80, 83,
  85–94
drug withdrawal, 66, 67
drug-trafficking organizations.
  See names of individual cartels

Escobar, Pablo, 19

"Fast and Furious," 69–70
Feeley, John D., 50
Félix Gallardo, Miguel Ángel
  (*el Padrino*), 17–19, 21
Fischbach, Michelle, 47
Focus on the Family, 76
Fox, Vicente, 27

INDEX CONTINUED

GAFE, 29, 30
García, Rico, 17
García Simental, Teodoro
 (*el Teo*), 23
Gilbride, John, 67
Gómez Palacio prison, 49
González Calderoni,
 Guillermo, 17
Guadalajara cartel, 19, 21
Gulf cartel, 30, 32, 78
Gutwillig, Stephen, 90
Guzmán Loera, Joaquín
 (*el Chapo*), 23–24, 60
Guzmán Pérez, Fernando, 51

Hakim, Julián, 42–44
hepatitis C, 66
heroin, 10, 11, 65–67, 77, 84
hostage negotiation, 40, 42
human immunodeficiency
 virus, 66, 91
human trafficking, 31, 75

*International Narcotics Control Strategy
 Report, The*, 50

Jesús Gutiérrez Rebollo, José
 de, 48–49
Jiménez, David, 60
Jiménez, Lina Erika, 58–59
Jiménez Lugo, Edgar (*el Ponchis*),
 55, 57–60
Jiménez Lugo, Elizabeth,
 58–59
Jiménez Lugo, Yolanda, 59
José Soriano, Juan, 6–9
Juárez cartel, 49

kidnappings, 23, 29, 30,
 36–44, 76
 express, 38, 42–43
 ransoms, 23, 38, 39, 40, 42
 virtual, 38–39
Kilmer, Beau, 92
Kirby, John, 23

la Banda de la Flor, 39
la Familia, 14, 34, 40
la mordida, 47
Lala Pomavilla, Luis Freddy, 29
Leija, Guadalupe, 60
López, Humberto, 69
los Palillos, 76
los Zetas, 29–31, 32, 34, 49
LSD, 84

Mafia, 30–31, 75, 78
Majera, Rodolfo, 49–50
Maketa, Terry, 78
Malverde, Jesús, 17
marijuana, 7, 8, 10, 17, 18, 65,
 76, 79, 84, 87, 89, 90–92
Marinol, 91
Martí, Alejandro, 39, 40
Martí, Fernando, 39, 40
May, Daniel, 77
McDermott, Donald, 9
Medellín cartel, 19
Méndez Santiago, Flavio
 (*el Amarillo*), 31
Merida Initiative, 71–72
methamphetamine, 10, 31, 65,
 77, 84, 90
Mexican Mafia, 75
Moreira, Humberto, 44

Moreno González, Nazario
(*el Más Loco*), 14, 34

Najera, Ricardo, 50
narco messages, 22
narcocorridos, 55
narcos, 7, 12, 14, 32
'Ndrangheta, 78
North American Free Trade
Agreement, 26–27

Obama, Barack, 93
O'Keefe, Kevin, 75
Operación Limpieza, 51
opium, 11, 17, 18
Ortiz Juárez, Sergio, 40

Padilla, Julio (*el Negro*), 59
Palma, Héctor (*el Guero*), 60
paraquat, 18
Partido Revolucionario
Institucional, 27
Paschall, James, 75
Peñalosa, Donaldo, 7
Percy, Charles, 18
Piña Ibarra, Raúl Gustavo, 32
Prohibition, 86
Project Gunrunner, 68–69
Proposition 19, 91–92
protective services, 42

Ramírez Mandujano, Noé, 51
Rand Corporation, 91, 92
Ravelo, Ricardo, 60
Reyes, Ralph, 30
Rojas Rodríguez, Margarita, 50
Rojas-López, Jorge, 76

Rojas-López, Victor, 76

Salmones, Cristián, 39, 40
Sánchez Arellano, Fernando
(*el Ingeniero*), 21–22, 23
Shirk, David, 21
SIEDO, 51
Sinaloa cartel, 23, 24, 51, 71
South Pacific cartel, 56, 57, 59
Speaking Out Against Drug Legalization,
88
Special Forces, US, 29
Stamper, Norm, 86–87

Taliban, 11
tapados, 32
Tirado, Carlos, 66
tourism in Mexico, 69
Tree, Sanho, 28–29

weapons, 10, 14, 29, 72, 74
AK-47 assault rifles, 9, 14, 71
gun laws, 43
smuggling, 68–71
"straw buying," 71
WikiLeaks, 50

Ye Gon, Zhenli, 31

Zambada García, Ismael
(*el Mayo*), 23

ABOUT THE AUTHOR

Courtney Farrell is a full-time writer and the author of numerous books for young people. She is interested in wildlife conservation, social justice, and sustainability issues. She lives with her husband and teenaged sons on a ranch in Colorado.

PHOTO CREDITS